Exploration
Into
AFRICA

ISIMEME IBAZEBO

new
Discovery
B·O·O·K·S
NEW YORK

First American publication 1994 by New Discovery Books, Macmillan Publishing Company, 866 Third Avenue, New York, NY 10022

Macmillan Publishing Company is part of the Maxwell Communication Group of Companies.

Library of Congress Cataloging-in-Publication Data

Ibazemo, Isimeme
    Exploration into Africa/Isimeme Ibazemo
        p.   cm.
    Includes index.
    ISBN 0-02-718081-6
    1. Africa—Discovery and exploration—European—Juvenile literature. 2. Europe—Exploring expeditions—Juvenile literature.   [1. Africa—Discovery and exploration.]
    I. Title.
DT3.12   1994
960—dc20

SUMMARY: An explanation of discoveries made in Africa, from the beginnings of time up to the 19th century explorers, with a postscript about modern Africa.

First published in Great Britain in 1994 by
Belitha Press Limited, 31 Newington Green, London N16 9PU

Printed in Hong Kong for Imago

Photographic credits

The Ancient Art and Architecture Collection 45 right; Bruce Coleman Limited 22 top; Gerald Cubitt Robert Estall Photographs 11 left; E.T. Archive 17 bottom, 21 bottom, 26, 40 top; Mary Evans Picture Library 14, 33 left, 38 right, 39 left; Werner Forman Archive Limited 6 bottom; Lagos Museum, Nigeria, 15, 16 bottom, 35 left; The Fotomas Index 9 top, 22 bottom, 24 bottom, 31 right; Giraudon 11 right, 24 top left, 32 top; Sonia Halliday Photographs 6 top, 7 right, 21 top; Robert Harding Picture Library front cover, 6 middle, 28 bottom; Hulton Deutsch Collection Limited 10, 16 top, 25, 40 bottom, 41, 42 right; The Hutchison Library 8, 9 bottom, 19 top, 30 bottom, 33 right, 42 left, 44; The Mansell Collection Limited back cover, 2, 17, top, 24 top right, 28 top, 30 middle, 31 left, 34 left, 35 right, 37 right; Peter Newark's Historical Pictures 30 top; Royal Geographical Society Picture Library title page, 7 left, 20 bottom, 32 bottom, 36, 37 left, 38 left, 39 right, 45 left; Dr Kevin Shillington 13; Syndication International 20 top, 34 right; Zefa Picture Library UK Limited 3, 23

Editor: Jill Laidlaw
Designer: Andrew Oliver
Picture researcher: Vanessa Kelly
Series consultant: Shane Winser,
Royal Geographical Society, London
Consultants: Dorothy Middleton, formerly
            of the Royal Geographical
            Society, London
            Dr. Kevin Shillington

The moment at which Henry Morton Stanley finds Dr David Livingstone four years after his disappearance. It was at this point that Stanley uttered the famous words 'Dr Livingstone, I presume?'.

Contents

A *modern-day Masai man from East Africa*

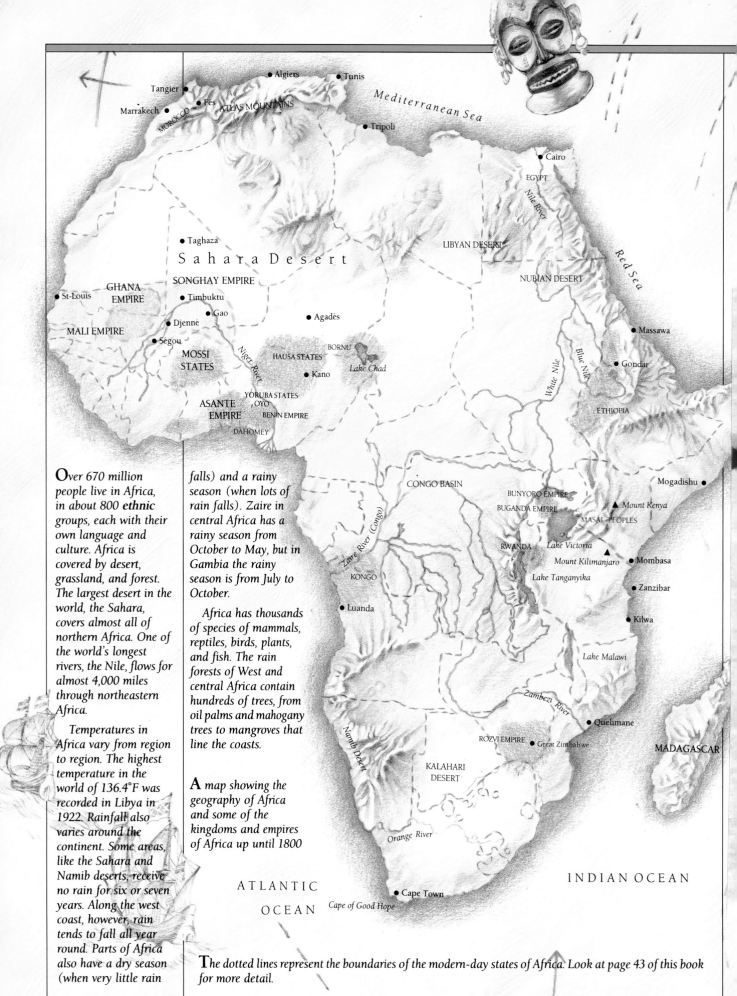

Over 670 million people live in Africa, in about 800 **ethnic** groups, each with their own language and culture. Africa is covered by desert, grassland, and forest. The largest desert in the world, the Sahara, covers almost all of northern Africa. One of the world's longest rivers, the Nile, flows for almost 4,000 miles through northeastern Africa.

Temperatures in Africa vary from region to region. The highest temperature in the world of 136.4°F was recorded in Libya in 1922. Rainfall also varies around the continent. Some areas, like the Sahara and Namib deserts, receive no rain for six or seven years. Along the west coast, however, rain tends to fall all year round. Parts of Africa also have a dry season (when very little rain falls) and a rainy season (when lots of rain falls). Zaire in central Africa has a rainy season from October to May, but in Gambia the rainy season is from July to October.

Africa has thousands of species of mammals, reptiles, birds, plants, and fish. The rain forests of West and central Africa contain hundreds of trees, from oil palms and mahogany trees to mangroves that line the coasts.

A map showing the geography of Africa and some of the kingdoms and empires of Africa up until 1800

The dotted lines represent the boundaries of the modern-day states of Africa. Look at page 43 of this book for more detail.

1 Exploring Africa

The Story of Africa

African history is fascinating. We have all heard about the great pharaohs of Egypt, with their magnificent tombs and burial ceremonies. But how many of us know about the ancient empires of West Africa? The first of these great kingdoms, Ghana, was powerful from A.D. 300 for about a thousand years (see page 8). Ghana was so rich that the dogs in the king's palace wore collars made out of gold.

Arab Scholars

In the tenth century, Arab **scholars** began to write about the great wealth of the African kingdoms. Some of them, such as Ibn Battuta (see pages 14–15), actually traveled around the continent. Others just gathered stories from those who had been to Africa.

As more books about Africa appeared, the fame of the kingdoms spread and Europeans began to visit the continent. First came the Portuguese in the 1400s. Then other Europeans such as the French, Dutch, and British followed. They built forts along the coast and traded with the Africans. But few Europeans actually traveled into the heart of the country and because they knew so little about Africa they called it the Dark Continent.

Exploring This Book

This book is divided into four sections. The first section deals with the history of Africa to the 1400s, and the second section takes the history up to the 1800s. Within each time period, we deal with different regions of Africa separately. The last two sections deal with European explorers who visited Africa from the late 1700s onward and Africa as it is today.

This book is the story of Africa and her visitors.

The Beginnings of History

The Stone Age

Scientists now believe that the very first human beings lived in Africa two million years ago. Because the early humans used stone tools as hunting weapons, this period of history is known as the Stone Age. People lived in small groups, moving about from place to place in search of food. People lived in this way for many thousands of years (until about 10,000 years ago). Stone Age people learned how to farm and keep animals. They started building permanent homes, growing rice and wheat and other grains, and keeping goats, sheep, and cattle for food. Their numbers increased because there was enough food to feed everyone. They even built fires to keep themselves warm.

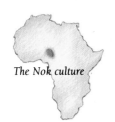

The Nok culture

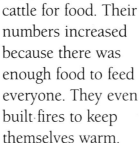

The Nok culture in western Africa lasted from about 500 B.C. to A.D. 200. The people of Nok made beautiful terra-cotta sculptures of human heads and animals.

The Iron Age

The next great discovery was how to make tools and weapons out of iron. Iron hoes and axes were much stronger than the old stone ones and could be used to clear large areas of land for farming. This period is known as the Iron Age and first developed in Africa from about 6000 B.C.

An ancient Egyptian wall painting in a tomb

Early Civilizations

Ancient Egypt was one of the world's first great civilizations. It developed along the banks of the Nile River around 3000 B.C. and flourished for over 2,000 years. The Egyptians produced the first 365-day calendar, developed basic arithmetic, and invented a form of picture writing called hieroglyphics. They built great temples and buried their rulers in massive tombs called pyramids. Ancient Egypt survived longer than any other known civilization and even conquered Nubia, a region of the upper Nile. Around 1000 B.C., the Nubians broke away and formed their own kingdom, which was called Kush. The Kushite civilization survived until A.D. 350 and was a center of art, learning, and trade.

The Trans-Saharan Trade

As more and more food was produced, people began to have special jobs. Some of them were responsible for providing food, while others just made tools and weapons. In time, people who lived in one community began to sell any extra goods they had to neighbors. Some people traveled over great distances to trade. The North African **Berbers** traveled south across the desert to sell goods to the people of West Africa. Because the Berbers traveled through the Sahara Desert, this trading became known as the trans-Saharan trade. No one knows when this trading began; some people say that as long as there have been people in Africa there has been trade.

Journeying through the Desert

The trans-Saharan trade thrived for over 2,000 years, only decreasing in the last century. The Berbers loaded up about 1,000 camels and traveled 1,500 miles across the desert. The journey usually took three months to complete and was fraught with dangers. Some merchants lost their way in the vast desert and died of thirst. Others got caught up in fierce sandstorms. When they finally got to the trading towns south of the desert, the Berbers **bartered** their salt and copper for gold and **kola nuts**.

The Growth of Empires

The people who lived at each end of the trans-Saharan trade routes were very fortunate. They were able to take part in the lucrative trade and become rich. Towns and villages began to select kings and form themselves into states. As trade expanded, the states grew even more powerful and started to conquer their weaker neighbors. Eventually, the states south of the Sahara grew into large and wealthy empires such as Ghana and Mali.

A *camel train crossing the Sahara Desert in southern Algeria*

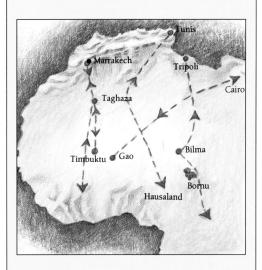

Routes across the Sahara

At the height of the trans-Saharan trade, there were three main routes that crossed the desert and ended at important trading cities. One route was from Marrakech to the salt mines of Taghaza. From there salt and copper were carried to the ancient Ghanaian Empire and Timbuktu. The second route ran from Tunis to Hausaland and Gao. The last one went from Tripoli to the salt mines of Bilma and then on to the ancient Bornu Empire. Both of these routes carried salt and copper. Salt was very important as it was used for cooking and for preserving meat in the hot climate. There were other secondary routes that crossed the main ones. For example, there was a **caravan** trail all the way from Cairo in the east to Gao in the west.

Salt pans in the Sahara at Teguidda, Niger

2 Africa to the 1400s

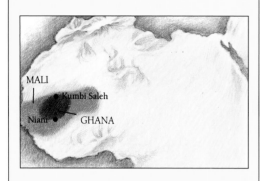

The Land of Gold

Ghana was the first great empire in West Africa. It began as a small state in the A.D. 300s and lasted for almost a thousand years. The capital of Ghana, Kumbi Saleh, had a population of about 15,000 people. The city was divided into two areas. The king lived in one section, in a palace built out of stone and decorated with paintings and carvings. His subjects also lived in this area, but their homes were built out of mud. Muslims who took part in the trans-Saharan trade lived in the other section of the city. They built houses and mosques for themselves out of stone.

The people of Ghana were farmers. They worshiped many gods and believed that people continued to live as spirits when they died. When a king of Ghana died, the people built a special hut for him. They put comfortable rugs on the floor for him to lie on and placed food, water, and his servants in the hut. The hut was then covered up with sand, burying the servants alive.

Ghana became wealthy because it lay at the southern end of the trans-Saharan trade route. Many Arab travelers visited the kingdom, and it became known as the Land of Gold.

Western Empires

The trans-Saharan trade continued to grow in volume up until the 1600s. The trade was very important to the West Africans, for not only did it bring new ideas but it brought the new religion of Islam from the north. The wealth of the trade helped some people to set up very powerful empires. Two of the most famous were Ghana (see box) and Mali.

The Growth of Kangaba

Mali started off as a small state called Kangaba. Then, in 1235, a great warrior, Sundiata, became ruler and founded the empire of Mali. The first thing he did was to build a new capital city at Niani where all his subjects could meet him. Sundiata sent his armies out to conquer areas in the south that mined gold and Taghaza in the north, which produced salt. Eventually, Sundiata controlled all the trans-Saharan trade in the area and Berbers flocked to his city to exchange their goods.

The bustling market at Djenné, with the old mosque (see page 9) in the background

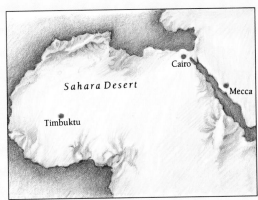

A *European map dated around 1375, showing the king and kingdom of Mali*

Mansu Musa's Pilgrimage

After Sundiata's death, Mali continued to be powerful. Many good rulers followed Sundiata and enlarged the empire. The next great ruler was Mansu Kankan Musa, who came to power in 1312. He made Mali wealthier by conquering the prosperous cities of Timbuktu and Gao.

Mansu Kankan Musa made his famous pilgrimage to Mecca from 1324 to 1326. Mecca is the holy city in Arabia that every follower of the **Muslim** faith (see box) is supposed to visit at least once during his lifetime. Mansu's pilgrimage made Mali known throughout the Mediterranean world. Mansu Musa took 60,000 servants, 100 camels, and a huge amount of gold with him on his trip across the desert. He gave a lot of his money away as gifts. Wherever Mansu stopped on a Friday, the Muslim day of worship, he gave the people who lived there money to build a mosque. Mosques are like churches. Muslims go there to pray to their god, Allah. Mansu Musa was so generous that he ended up having to borrow money from an Egyptian merchant to get back home.

Timbuktu, the Islamic Center

Mansu Musa brought architects and scholars back with him from Egypt. He asked architects to build Islamic schools in Timbuktu. He also encouraged Muslim scholars from other countries to come and live in the city. By the end of his reign in 1337, Timbuktu had become a famous center of Islamic learning.

The Birth of Islam

In A.D. 622, the Prophet Muhammad founded a new religion in Arabia, called Islam. The people who follow it are called Muslims and they believe in one god whom they call Allah.

The first Muslims wanted to convert other peoples who did not believe in their religion. After the Prophet Muhammad died in 632, his followers began to wage wars against people who lived in other countries. They conquered Egypt in 639 and most of North Africa by the 700s.

Muslims follow a holy book called the Koran. It contains passages that tell them how to live a good life. Muslims are supposed to pray five times a day, give food or money to the poor, **fast** during **Ramadan**, and make a pilgrimage to Mecca at least once in their lifetime. There are more than one billion Muslims in the world and 150 million of them live in Africa.

The elegant Sultan Haman Mosque in Cairo, Egypt

Moving East

While some people were forming empires in the west, others were **migrating** to other parts of Africa. These people spoke several languages called Bantu, and they started migrating over 4,000 years ago. The Bantus moved into the forests of central Africa, continuing until they reached the East African coast around A.D. 400.

Across the Indian Ocean

The Bantu-speaking Africans who settled along the coast were farmers who kept cattle and grew crops. In due course, they also traded across the Indian Ocean with Arabia, Persia, and India. Merchants from these countries had learned how to sail on the **monsoon** winds, which blew from India toward East Africa between November and March. They brought goods such as beads, plates, and silk from China and India to sell at East African ports. The Africans sold ivory and gold, which they bought from people living in the **interior**. When the monsoon winds blew eastward between April and October, the foreign merchants sailed home in their **dhows**.

A detail from a 19th-century European engraving of an Arab caravan traveling across the desert to sell its wares

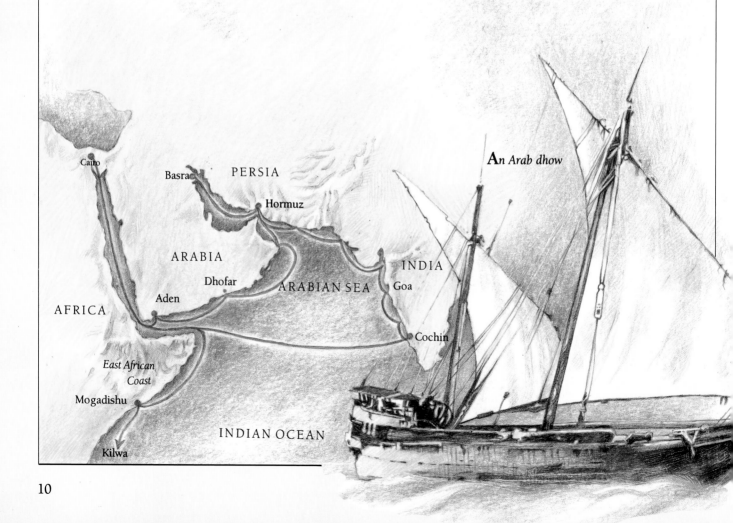

An Arab dhow

Cairo
Basra
PERSIA
Hormuz
ARABIA
Dhofar
ARABIAN SEA
Aden
AFRICA
INDIA
Goa
Cochin
East African Coast
Mogadishu
Kilwa
INDIAN OCEAN

A *Swahili man blowing on a Siwa horn. Swahilis are the descendants of Bantu and Arab settlers.*

A *page from Ptolemy's book* Geography

Arab Settlers

During the tenth century, Arab merchants began to settle along the East African coast. They learned the languages and became middlemen, buying goods from Africans who lived farther inland and selling them to the sea merchants. A century later, wars in Persia and Arabia forced many Arabs to move away from their troubled homes. Some of them ended up settling along the East African coast and taking part in the trade as well. These Arabs married local African women, and as time went on a new language called Swahili developed. Swahili is basically a Bantu language with lots of Arabic words. It is still spoken today throughout eastern Africa and is the national language of Tanzania and Kenya.

Growing Settlements

Many Arab immigrants settled in the port of Mogadishu, and it became an important center of the Indian Ocean trade. But as the demand for African ivory (elephant tusks) increased in China and India, more Arabs left Persia and Oman and settled along the East African coast. Finally, in the 12th century, a number of Swahili merchants who lived in the north moved to the south and established new trading cities. The most important and wealthy city was Kilwa. Kilwa controlled the Indian Ocean trade in the south of Africa. Most of the houses in the city were built out of **coral**, and there was a huge palace that covered almost one **hectare**. The Muslims of Kilwa built many fine mosques out of stone and made their own copper and silver coins. Kilwa's power lasted until the 15th century when quarrels between ruling families led to its decline.

The Earliest Books

Over 2,000 years ago, a Greek merchant wrote a guide for seamen called the *Periplus Maris Erythraei (Voyage around the Indian Ocean)*. It describes the ports along the East African coast and the trade that took place between African and overseas merchants. The author of the book wrote about a rich, southerly port called Rhapta, where there was plenty of ivory and tortoiseshell. Archaeologists have failed to uncover this site, but they think it may be somewhere in modern Tanzania.

In the fifth century B.C., a book came out that described the East African trading ports. It was written by the Egyptian geographer and astronomer Ptolemy, and was called *Geography*. After Ptolemy's book, not much was written about the east coast until Arab geographers started visiting it more than 400 years later.

Great Zimbabwe

Great Zimbabwe

While Arabs were settling at Kilwa on the east coast, another Bantu city was being built farther inland in southeastern Africa. It was called Great Zimbabwe. Great Zimbabwe was important for Indian Ocean trade because most of the gold and ivory sold by Arab merchants at Sofala (a port on the coast) passed through the city.

The Stone Walls

Bantu-speaking people started living around the **Zimbabwean Plateau** about 1,500 years ago. The early settlers lived on the hill and were farmers who kept cattle. Then, in the 1200s, the Bantu people built a massive stone wall to surround their settlement. The wall was made out of granite, a local stone that cracks into pieces at night after a hot, sunny day.

A century later, the ruler moved from the hill to the valley and founded Great Zimbabwe. It consisted of a house for the ruler with many other huts for members of the royal family surrounding it. All the homes were made out of thick clay and covered in designs. Each house had its own stone wall surrounding it. There were also courtyards and areas where people could cook. Soon after 1300, a great stone wall ten yards high was built to protect the whole area.

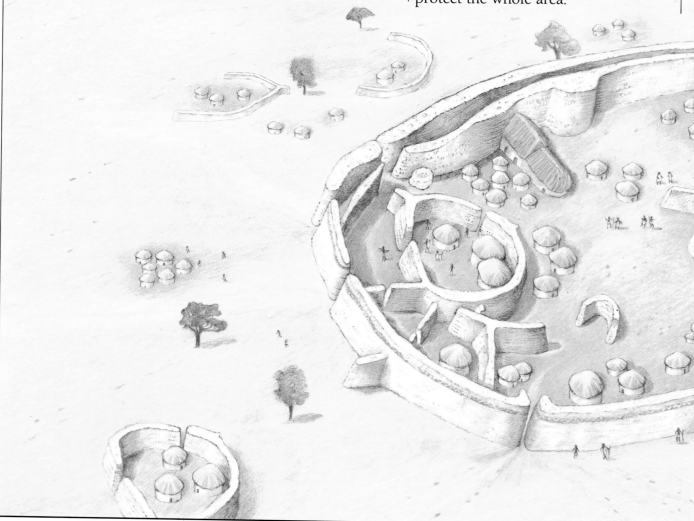

People of the Valley

About 10,000 people lived outside the stone walls of Great Zimbabwe and they all had different jobs. Some were herders who moved their cattle from one grazing ground to another. Others were craftspeople who made jewelry out of gold and copper. Sculptors carved in wood and stone, and locally grown cotton enabled weavers to make fine cloth. But the most important people were the traders who carried gold and ivory to the east coast. Great Zimbabwe did not have any metals of its own, so people had to get copper from mines in the north and gold from people in the south. It was this trade that made Great Zimbabwe one of the most powerful kingdoms of Africa in the 1300s.

End of the Kingdom

The stone walls of Great Zimbabwe were a symbol of power and wealth that also gave people privacy. However, in the mid-1400s, Great Zimbabwe was suddenly burned down and abandoned. No one knows why this was done. But the stone walls were so well built that they still survive today as a reminder of the ancient power of Great Zimbabwe.

A *modern-day picture of the ruins of Great Zimbabwe (left). The drawing at the bottom is a construction of Great Zimbabwe at its height during the 1400s. Although the walls were tall and powerful, they were not built for defense. Instead, they were built to enhance the power of the king.*

3 Visitors and Traders

The Traveler of Islam

Even before Great Zimbabwe was mysteriously abandoned, an amazing man was making his way acrosss Africa, Asia, and the Middle East. His name was Ibn Battuta and he was the greatest Arab traveler of his time. When Ibn Battuta was only 21 (in 1325), he started his journey. By the time he finally returned to his country 29 years later, he had traveled 74,000 miles. This earned him the title "Traveler of Islam." Before Ibn Battuta visited West Africa, he traveled through Asia for 23 years. At first he only wanted to visit the holy city of Mecca. However, one night, he dreamed that a bird had taken him to a dark, green country—the Orient —and so began his adventures.

Through the Sahara

Ibn Battuta returned to Morocco in 1348 and then left again in 1349 to visit Spain and the famous empire of Mali (see pages 8–9). With enough food to last four months, he traveled through the vast Sahara Desert with some North African merchants who were on their way south to trade. It took the party just two months to reach Walata, the northernmost city of Mali. Ibn Battuta was tired so he stayed there for 50 days, resting and eating pounded **millet** mixed with milk and honey.

Ibn Battuta's Adventures

Ibn Battuta spent 23 years traveling through the Middle East, India, and China. He visited the tombs of Abraham, Isaac, and Jacob at Bethlehem. He sailed down the east coast of Africa, spending time at the commercial ports of Mogadishu and Kilwa. While he was in Delhi (India), he was made a judge by the sultan. By the time Ibn Battuta returned to Morocco in 1348, he had traveled through 44 of the countries we know today.

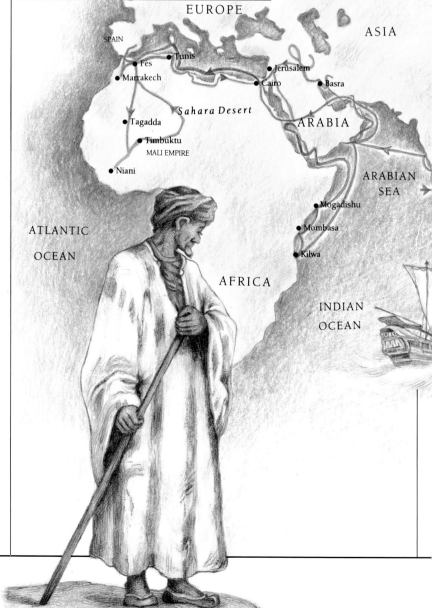

EUROPE

ASIA

SPAIN

Fes • • Tunis

Marrakech • • Jerusalem

Cairo • • Basra

Sahara Desert

ARABIA

Tagadda •

Timbuktu •
MALI EMPIRE

Niani •

ARABIAN SEA

ATLANTIC OCEAN

Mogadishu •

Mombasa •

Kilwa •

AFRICA

INDIAN OCEAN

On to Niani

Ibn Battuta's next task was to get to Niani, the capital of Mali. This time he traveled with a guide and three companions. Unfortunately, when he finally arrived at the capital in June 1352, he fell ill and was bedridden for two months. When he recovered, Ibn Battuta met the king Mansa Sulayman. But he was very disappointed with the gifts the king gave him. Ibn Battuta had heard stories about the previous kings of Mali, and how generous they were with their gold. So the bread and beef Mansa Sulayman sent him seemed miserly in comparison.

Back to Morocco

On February 27, 1353, Ibn Battuta left Niani. He passed through Timbuktu, sailed down the Niger River, and saw a hippopotamus for the first time. After resting for a month at Gao, a prosperous city on the Niger, he crossed the desert with a large caravan of merchants. Ibn Battuta spent a few days at the city of Tagadda, and the local sultan sent him and his party two roasted rams every day to eat. On September 11, Ibn Battuta set off again. He finally arrived back at Fez, Morocco, in February 1354.

Writing Rihla

Ibn Battuta's travels were not in vain. When he got back to Fez, he spent the following two years working on his book called *Rihla*. He worked with a poet called Ibn Juzayy, who took down all his notes. After the book was finished, Ibn Battuta spent the rest of his years acting as a judge. He died in 1369 at the age of 64.

Travelers and Scholars

Ibn Battuta was not the only Arab to travel around Africa. Al-Masudi sailed down the east coast of Africa in about A.D. 922. He wrote about the trade between the people of the east coast, India, and China. The Arab scholar and geographer al-Idrisi was born in North Africa in 1100. He traveled when he was a young man, and wrote about the wealthy Ghanaian Empire. A later traveler, Mahmud Kati, was born in Timbuktu in 1468. He accompanied the king of Mali to Mecca and later wrote about his experiences.

Not all the Arab writers actually traveled to Africa. For example, although al-Bakri wrote about West Africa, he never left his hometown in Spain. Instead, he collected stories from Muslim merchants who had been there.

Sometimes the writers exaggerated in their books. Al-Hamadhani's book, which appeared in the ninth century, said Ghana was "a country where gold grows like plants in the sand, in the same way as carrots do, and is plucked at sunset."

A *well-dressed Fulah woman at Mopti in Mali*

The Europeans Arrive

Over 100 years after Ibn Battuta's death, the Portuguese reached the coast of West Africa. They established forts along the coast to trade with people, exchanging weapons, metal utensils, and cloth for ivory, gold, and pepper. Christopher Columbus sailed from Spain and unwittingly reached the West Indies in 1492. Eight years later, a Portuguese captain landed in Brazil.

The Slave Trade

The Americas were full of gold and silver, and the land was ideal for sugar **plantations**. Many Spanish settlers moved there to mine the land and grow sugar. They forced the Native Americans to do all the mining and farming, and almost 90 percent of them died from hardship and disease. European criminals who were sent to work the land fared no better, and were soon dying from **tropical diseases**. To solve the problem, the settlers began to transport slaves from West Africa to work on the land.

The Expansion of the Trade

As the slave trade continued, Spanish settlements spread out all over Central and South America. Other European nations noticed the profit being made from the slave trade and soon joined in. The English set up trading posts along the West African coast in 1553, and the Dutch in 1593. By the 17th century, the number of Africans shipped across the Atlantic to the Americas was a staggering 1.8 million. The Africans were taken against their will, captured either during slave raids, or after wars between African kingdoms. Chained together like cattle, they were led to the coast and sold to slave merchants. Their long, terrible experience was just beginning.

From the late 1400s onward, many European merchants built trading castles along the West African coast. Cape Coast Castle (below) was Britain's main trading fort along the Gold Coast. It was built in the 1600s.

As early as the 900s, Arabs developed a profitable slave trade of their own on the East African coast. The Africans in the picture are being led to Kilwa, the center of the Arab slave trade.

The Results of the Trade

Over 12 million Africans were captured and taken to the Americas during the 400 years of the slave trade (1490s–1880s). The European merchants and plantation owners who took part benefited greatly. The farmers grew crops such as sugar, cotton, and tobacco on the wide expanse of American land and lived in splendid mansions. The merchants made huge profits on each of their journeys. The remaining Africans were sold guns, which they used against one another. The imported goods that the Africans received could not make up for the loss of people. The Africans who were taken as slaves were the most important ones —the young.

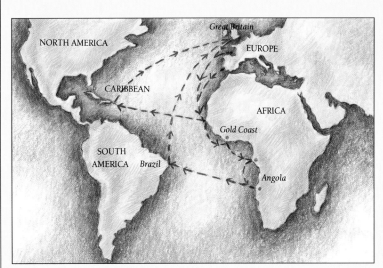

The Triangle Trade

The transatlantic slave trade was called the triangle trade because of the way it was organized. Merchants sailed from European ports in ships equipped with trading goods, iron shackles to chain people, feeding bowls, and whips. They also took special chisels, which they used to knock out the front teeth of those who tried to starve themselves to death. The merchants tried to fit as many Africans as possible onto the ships, and some people even had to lie on top of each other. The journey across the Atlantic was called the middle passage. It took three to six weeks and was a horrible trip. Africans died by the thousands because of poor sanitation. Packed together like sardines below deck, any disease that occurred spread very quickly. When the ships finally reached the Americas, the Africans were sold to wealthy plantation owners. The merchants then took sugar, gold, silver, tobacco, rice, ginger, and cotton back with them to Europe. The reason the slave trade lasted for so long was because it was very profitable. For example, one particular merchant from Liverpool (England) made a profit of over $3 million in just four years.

This cross section of a slave ship shows how tightly Africans were packed together. On the right, guns are used to stop Africans from rebelling on a slave ship. This did not stop many Africans from jumping overboard and swimming for freedom.

Kingdoms of the Guinea Coast

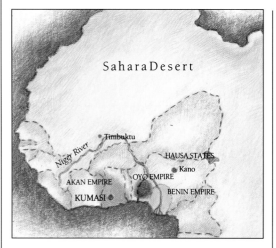

With the arrival of European merchants along the coast, many African kingdoms became rich and powerful. They bought guns from the merchants and waged wars on one another to try and enlarge their empires.

The Oyo and Benin kingdoms (15th to 18th centuries) are famous for their bronze works of art. Farther west, the Akan people formed a number of kingdoms of their own, the most famous of which was called Asante. The Asante Empire lasted for over 150 years, and when it was at its most powerful, five million people lived in it.

The Beginnings of the Asante Empire

The Akan people once lived around western Sudan. Then, a thousand years ago, they migrated to the south and settled around the Pra and Ofin rivers. As the area became more crowded, a family called Oyoko moved away to the north and built a small town, which they called Asantemanso. As time went by, the Akan people built more towns, each with its own ruler. One of these new towns was called Kumasi. When Osei Tutu became king of Kumasi in 1680, he united all the separate towns and called his new empire Asante.

Drawings of some Asante (Ghana) jewelry

A small bronze statue measuring about 18 inches from the ancient Benin Empire in West Africa

Buying Gold and Making Art

Osei Tutu made the capital of his empire Kumasi. It was a large and important city and many Muslim scholars and diplomats from other parts of Africa lived there. Merchants came all the way from towns in northern Africa, such as Timbuktu and Kano, to buy gold and kola nuts in Kumasi. The Asante also bought goods from merchants along the coast. The Asante Empire became very wealthy and even developed its own system of weights to measure gold dust. Asante craftspeople became famous for their beautiful carvings and sculptures in wood, silver, and gold.

Osei Tutu started a religious festival that took place once a year. The festival was called Odwira. Every year, all the different rulers within the empire gathered at the capital, Kumasi, and worshiped their ancestors and gods. They also pledged their support to the king. This festival is still celebrated today and elders wear gold tablets on their heads to signify their importance.

Great Kings

Osei Tutu ruled over Asante until 1717. Then his grandnephew, Opoku Ware, became king. Opoku Ware was a warrior, and in the 30 years of his reign, he made the Asante Empire even larger. The next two great Asante leaders had a massive empire to govern. They organized a strong government with officers to collect taxes throughout the region. But by the end of the 1800s, the empire began to grow weaker. It was involved in many wars with people along the coast. It also fought nine battles with the British between 1807 and 1901. By the end of these battles, the British had gained control of the Asante Empire.

Most of the bronze heads of the Benin Empire were made in honor of kings who were called obas. This head of the queen mother is 20 inches high.

The Golden Stool

When Osei Tutu became king of Kumasi, he was advised by his friend Okomfo Anokye. Okomfo introduced the Golden Stool into Asante life. The stool was made out of wood and was partly covered with gold. The stool was supposed to unite all the people in the empire under one symbol, rather like a flag. The people of Asante believed the stool had come down from heaven. They thought it represented the soul of the Asante people and that they had to guard it at all times.

A Warrior-Preacher

In the 1800s, Muslim scholars in western Africa began holy wars called jihads. The greatest leader of these wars was Usuman dan Fodio. As a young man, Usuman studied Islam and began to preach to the **Fulani** people in his homeland of Gobir. He won so many followers that the king of Gobir tried to have him killed, but Usuman and his followers escaped to Gudu in February 1804. In Gudu, he was made Leader of the Believers. This means he led all the people who believed in Islam (see page 9). Usuman launched wars against **pagans** and conquered his old homeland within six years. He then united all his conquests into one great empire, and divided it up between his brother and son. After his days of war, Usuman retired to dedicate his life to prayer and learning.

The Mighty Rozvi

The first Portuguese contacts with Africa were made at Sofala. This is a 17th-century European map of the trading post of Sofala with its fort, church, and houses.

Stone wall ruins such as these at Khami can be found all over the Zimbabwean Plateau.

The Rozvi Empire

While the British and Africans were busy trading and fighting on the west coast, the Portuguese sailed around the southern tip of Africa to the east coast. In the 1530s, they sent a party up the Zambezi River to find out where the gold sold by Swahili traders came from. They ended up establishing trading links with the Monomotapa Empire, a large inland empire in charge of much of the trade. By the 1600s, many more Portuguese settlers arrived in the area, taking over large areas of land and disrupting the Monomotapa Empire.

Dombo the Great

The Portuguese were prevented from moving farther inland by a man named Dombo. He was a wealthy cattle owner who set up his own empire in south-western Zimbabwe known as Rozvi. Between 1684 and 1696, Dombo and his army fought the Portuguese, and finally drove them off the Zimbabwean Plateau entirely. After Dombo died in 1696, the Rozvi Empire continued to expand.

Growth of the Empire

The Rozvi people built themselves a new capital at Khami. Their king took the title of mambo, and he ruled over the vast empire with the help of local chiefs and officials. The officials were in charge of collecting taxes in different areas—gold, ivory, cattle, and animal skins—which they took back to the mambo. The mambo had many wives, and some of them helped him to rule.

The people of Rozvi were traders, herders, and farmers. They grew crops such as pumpkins, beans, and watermelons and they used cattle for tilling the land. Traders moved around the empire selling local cloth, ivory, and beads and buying cannons and jewelry from the Portuguese.

Magic and Religion

The people of Rozvi believed in one god whom they called Mwari. He had a special place, or shrine, where people went to worship him. Priests looked after the shrines and they were the only ones allowed to talk directly to Mwari.

The Rozvi people also believed that their king had magical powers. Some said that he had a jug of oil that could kill any living person. A lot of them thought the mambo could make bees fight for him, make rain fall, and change the color of cattle.

End of Empire

The Rozvi Empire was brought to an end in the 1830s by an invasion of warring peoples from southern Africa, the Nguni. These wars spread out all over central and southern Africa, and lasted for over 15 years. They are known as the Mfecane, or "time of crushing."

A painting of the king Shaka by Gerard Bengu

Shaka, the Zulu Warrior

Shaka was the **illegitimate** son of the Zulu chief. When he was young, he joined a neighboring chief's army. He proved to be such a brave soldier that he was made commander of the army regiment. After Shaka's father died in 1816, he became ruler of Zululand.

Shaka enlarged Zululand by conquering many neighboring lands. He introduced new fighting methods into his army, and even arranged it into 15 regiments with special names and equipment. Whenever his army conquered a new land, his soldiers took all the women, children, young men, and cattle back with them to Zululand. Shaka then placed all the men in his regiments. He made each regiment carry shields of a certain color and wear special headscarves. Shaka even sent some members of the royal family to live in the barracks. Shaka died in 1828 when he was only 41. He was killed by his brothers, and one of them went on to become the new Zulu king.

An illustration of the Zulu king Mpande training his troops

21

Inside East Africa

Bunyoro
•
Buganda

BUNYORO

BUGANDA

Lake
Victoria

Lake
Tanganyika

Lake Malawi

Farther north, the kingdoms around the lakes of East Africa escaped the devastating effects of the Mfecane. But they were involved in wars of their own, raiding neighboring peoples and taking away their cattle and land. The two most powerful kingdoms were Bunyoro, which lay on the edge of Lake Albert, and Buganda on the edge of Lake Victoria.

An Expanding Kingdom

Bunyoro was the first kingdom to become important in this region. The main occupation of the people was cattle raising, but they also produced salt, which they sold to their neighbors. Bunyoro was divided into several villages, and each village provided men for the king's army. During the 16th and 17th centuries, the army conducted many raids against neighbors, seizing their cattle and land and making them pay taxes to the king.

A Rival Neighbor

Up until the middle of the 18th century, Bunyoro was the most powerful kingdom around the lakes. Then, in the 19th century, a kingdom that lay toward the east took over. It was called Buganda and over half a million Ganda people lived there.

The kingdom of Buganda lay on the northwestern shores of Lake Victoria. This view of the lake was taken from Kisumu in Kenya.

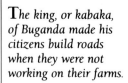

The king, or kabaka, of Buganda made his citizens build roads when they were not working on their farms.

Buganda lay on the shores of Lake Victoria, where the soil is very fertile. People grew crops such as bananas and plantains. Bananas were very easy to grow, and any rotten vegetables were used as fertilizers. Ganda people were also hunters who killed buffalo, antelope, and wild pigs. They attended regular markets, selling their crafts and crops in exchange for other goods.

Plantains are tropical vegetables that are related to the banana.

The king, or kabaka, divided Buganda into sections and appointed chiefs to rule over each area. The chiefs were responsible for collecting food, beer, and firewood from the people, which they took back to the king's court. Buganda also had trading links with Arab merchants on the east coast, and bought guns, ammunition, cotton cloth, beads, and glassware from them.

Ganda Religions

The Ganda believed that certain people in the kingdom had supernatural powers when they were alive. They called these people *balubaale*, and after they died people prayed to them for different things. One *balubaale* was in charge of bringing rain and another helped hunters find animals. There were also many medicine men who gave herbs and potions to people when they were ill.

Two Masai men of East Africa wearing traditional clothing. Masai men often undergo military training during their teenage years.

The Champion Nomads

The Masai are a group of African people who move around with their cattle in search of grazing land. Today they live in Tanzania and Kenya. The Masai were a small group of people in the 1500s, but by the 1800s the population had expanded greatly. The Masai men were in charge of moving cattle from place to place, while the women did all the milking. They believed in a supreme god called Enkai, and prayed to him through their religious leader. The leader also prayed for rain and made charms to protect soldiers going into battle.

The Chwezi

Bantu people living around the East African lakes were joined by a people called Chwezi in the 1300s. The Chwezi came from North Africa and were cattle herders. Before their arrival, the Bantu had lived in separate family groups, each with its own ruler. The Chwezi introduced the idea of a single ruler, or king, and encouraged the people to grow coffee. The Chwezi built long ditches, called *oriembo*, which they used to protect their cattle. They ruled over a large area, and their kingdom lasted 200 years.

5 Changing Times

From Slave Trade to Exploration

Jean-Jacques Rousseau was a French philosopher who was opposed to the slave trade. He believed that all human beings were equal and had a right to freedom.

Africans who were taken away as slaves often tried to escape, and there were many revolts on plantations in the Americas. The most dramatic revolt occurred in St. Dominique in 1791, when Toussaint L'Ouverture led Africans to fight against the French colonists—and won.

While kingdoms were rising and falling in eastern Africa, in Britain a new movement was growing to end the slave trade. There were many reasons why this happened.

The **Industrial Revolution** had begun during the second half of the 18th century. **Industrialists** wanted new markets and **raw materials** for their factories. Many factory owners realized that it would be better if Africans stayed in their countries to produce raw materials and buy products made in Europe.

Fighting for Freedom

There were several other groups of people who wanted the slave trade to end. **Humanitarians** in Europe and America campaigned against slavery. They collected stories from Africans about their sufferings and published them in books and newspapers. Churchmen called evangelists and writers such as the French philosopher Jean-Jacques Rousseau were also against the trade. In England, the fight against the slave trade was led by William Wilberforce. Africans who had gained their freedom joined the struggle, giving speeches about the horrors they had experienced at the hands of their owners.

The people who wanted to stop the slave trade tried to make people aware of how evil it was. They often printed leaflets like this one, which they distributed at their rallies.

A Great Campaigner

Olaudah Equiano was born in West Africa in 1745. When he was only nine years old, he was captured by slave traders and sold to Europeans on the coast. He was taken across the Atlantic Ocean in a slave ship. When Equiano arrived in Barbados, he was bought by an English naval captain. Finally, when he was 21, Equiano bought his freedom and began to travel alone. Between 1772 and 1780, he visited the Arctic, the Mediterranean, and Central America. In the 1780s, Equiano joined the antislavery movement in London. Equiano published a book in 1789 called *The Life of Olaudah Equiano,* which described his early life in Africa and the horrors of the slave trade. The book was very popular in Britain and America and was translated into Dutch, German, and Russian. After his book was published, Equiano traveled around England speaking against slavery and selling his book. He died in England on March 31, 1797.

The Kings' Letters

African kings who were against the slave trade did all they could to stop it. Some of them wrote letters to the governments of European countries. In 1526, the ruler of the Kingdom of Kongo sent a letter to the Portuguese king asking him to stop the slave trade. King Agaja of West Africa sent a similar letter to the British government in 1724. But European governments didn't reply, and the slave trade continued.

Warring Colonies

Africans who were still working on plantations were also fighting for their freedom. In Brazil, some African slaves escaped from a plantation and founded a republic of their own in 1605. It was called Palmares and survived for a hundred years before it was finally defeated by the Portuguese. In the French **colony** of St. Dominque, 400,000 Africans rebelled against the plantation owners in 1791. They defeated large French and British armies and established the independent republic of Haiti in 1803.

Finally, in 1807, the British government passed a law that made the slave trade illegal. But in reality it took over 50 years for the trade to stop completely. Plantation owners in North America continued buying slaves until 1865, and in South America, Argentina and Brazil did not stop until 1883.

The Explorers

Even though the European slave trade thrived for over 400 years, Europeans knew very little about the African continent. They knew about the coasts where their merchants often traded with Africans, but still had very little knowledge of the interior.

European industrialists wanted to know about the geography of Africa and the people who lived there, so that they could set up trading posts within the continent. Toward the end of the 18th century, explorers began to venture into the heart of Africa. They were sent by businessmen, Christian churches, geographical societies, and governments. Some explorers who were interested in the wildlife and geography of Africa used their own money to pay for their trips.

Young African children were forced to work on sugar plantations with their parents.

Why Explore Africa?

Mapping the Continent

By the early 1800s, most of the rivers, lakes, and mountains of the world were known to the Europeans. But one continent still remained a mystery—Africa. Between 1788 and 1877, there was at least one European expedition journeying into Africa every year. Some were searching for the **sources** of major rivers; others were looking for cities such as Timbuktu; while others were climbing mountains. Some explorers even traveled with Arab caravans through the desert, disguising themselves as Muslims to escape attack.

Commerce and Christianity

Missionaries like Dr. David Livingstone (see pages 36–39) wanted to find the main routes by river into Africa so that Europeans could easily move their goods into the heart of the country for trading. Dr. Livingstone thought that Christianity would be carried into the interior by European merchants and that the slave trade would end as a result. Unfortunately, this was rarely the case. Many European traders treated the Africans unfairly and it took many years to ban the slave trade.

Mining Africa

Africa is a land of outstanding natural beauty and contains many useful materials like minerals, gold, rubber, and **palm oil**. Europeans wanted to use many of these raw materials in their industries and came to Africa to get them.

Fame and Fortune

Many other Europeans wanted to explore Africa for very different reasons. Some wanted to write books about their travels and become famous, much as people still do today. Some people wanted to see the amazingly beautiful animals of Africa such as the elephant, the lion, and the giraffe. Many people came to examine the amazing plants, insects, and flowers of Africa and take them back to Europe where nothing else like them exists.

An illustration of Richard Burton wearing Arab clothes on his journey around East Africa. Many European travelers used this means of disguise to escape attack. Some of them even darkened their faces and learned the Arabic language. This was so they could blend in well with the local people on their long journeys.

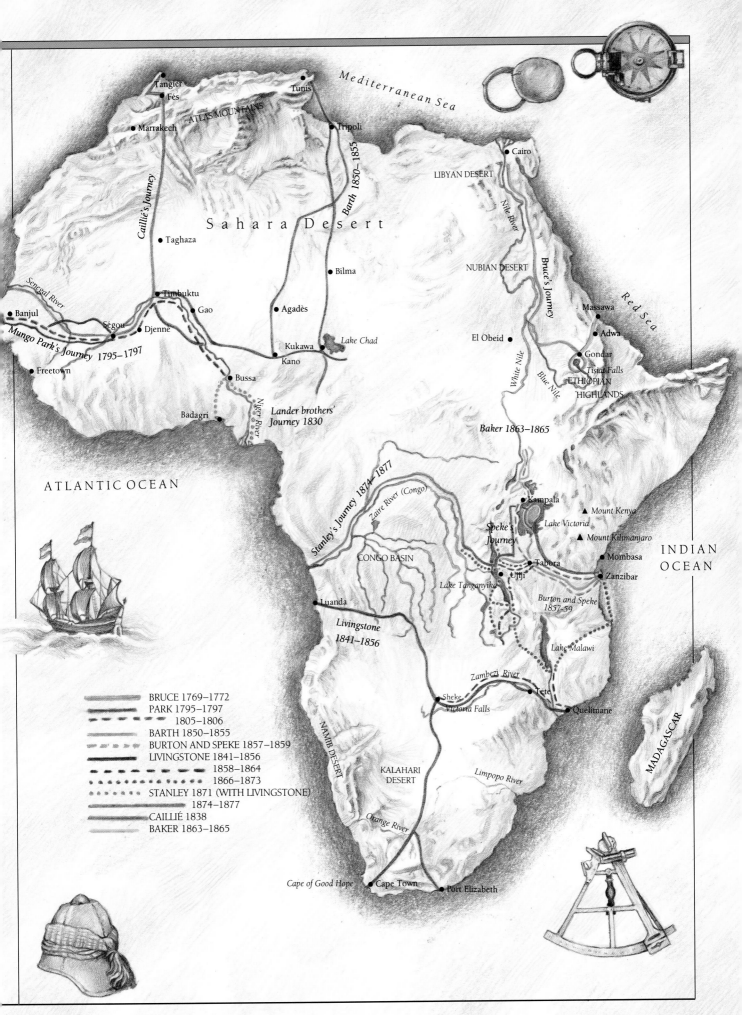

Mediterranean Sea

Tangier
Fés
ATLAS MOUNTAINS
Marrakech
Tunis
Tripoli
Cairo

LIBYAN DESERT

Caillié's Journey
Barth 1850–1855
Sahara Desert

Taghaza
Bilma
NUBIAN DESERT

Bruce's Journey

Senegal River
Timbuktu
Gao
Agadès
Massawa
Adwa

Banjul
Ségou
Djenné
Kukawa
Kano
Lake Chad
El Obeid
Gondar
Tisiat Falls
ETHIOPIAN
HIGHLANDS

Mungo Park's Journey 1795–1797

Freetown

Bussa

Badagri

Lander brothers'
Journey 1830

Niger River
White Nile
Blue Nile
Red Sea

Baker 1863–1865

ATLANTIC OCEAN

Stanley's Journey 1874–1877

Zaire River (Congo)
Kampala
Mount Kenya
Lake Victoria
Speke's
Journey
Mount Kilimanjaro

CONGO BASIN
Tabora
Mombasa
Ujiji
Zanzibar
Lake Tanganyika

Luanda
Burton and Speke
1857–59

Livingstone
1841–1856
Lake Malawi

INDIAN
OCEAN

Zambezi River
Tete

Sheke
Victoria Falls
Quelimane

MADAGASCAR

NAMIB DESERT

BRUCE 1769–1772
PARK 1795–1797
1805–1806
BARTH 1850–1855
BURTON AND SPEKE 1857–1859
LIVINGSTONE 1841–1856
1858–1864
1866–1873
STANLEY 1871 (WITH LIVINGSTONE)
1874–1877
CAILLIÉ 1838
BAKER 1863–1865

KALAHARI
DESERT
Limpopo River

Orange River

Cape of Good Hope
Cape Town
Port Elizabeth

27

6 Europeans into the Interior

In Search of the Nile

Nile River

A *portrait of James Bruce, the Scottish explorer who spent almost five years traveling around Ethiopia*

The beautiful Tisiat Falls that Bruce visited on his travels. Bruce stayed with the royal family in Gondar (below).

James Bruce was the first modern explorer to visit Ethiopia. He was born in 1730, and when he was young his father wanted him to become a lawyer, but Bruce hated the law and soon gave up his legal studies. Bruce worked in the London wine trade for a while and then in 1761 he became the British **consul** in Algeria. He found the place very dangerous and soon resigned from his post. He then spent some time traveling around North Africa and Syria, visiting historical buildings and noting their architecture. But Bruce had one burning ambition—to travel to Ethiopia, where he hoped to find the source of the Nile.

Into Ethiopia

Bruce arrived at Massawa, one of Ethiopia's ports, on September 19, 1769. Unfortunately for him, the Muslim ruler there was very unfriendly and even threatened to throw him into a dungeon. After being delayed for two months, Bruce was given a guide and two **bearers** to help him on his journey to Gondar. The party climbed over the steep Taranta Mountain and couldn't sleep at night because lions and hyenas prowled around their campsite. Bruce spent some time with the royal family at Gondar, meeting important people and attending wedding feasts. But he longed to continue his journey, so when the king's army set off to fight a rebel chief, he followed them as far as the Tisiat Falls (see left). He described them as the "most magnificent sight he had ever seen." Returning to Gondar, Bruce stayed with the royal family for some time. He finally set off for the Nile in October 1770.

On to the River

Bruce first of all visited the **provincial ruler** of the south to ask for his protection. The ruler gave him a guide and a horse and wished him a safe journey. The party headed south, passing beautiful **acacia trees** and splendidly colored birds. When Bruce reached Lake Tana at the **headwaters** of the Blue Nile on November 2, 1770, he was overjoyed and even offered a toast to his king, George III. But unfortunately, Bruce was mistaken. He did not know that the real source of the Nile lay many miles south, around Lake Victoria. The Blue Nile is a river that runs into the main river, known as the White Nile. Bruce spent five days measuring the river and making notes of the plants and animals. When he finished, he returned to Gondar.

Back through the Desert

On December 26, 1771, Bruce began his long return journey. He was chased by an elephant and almost died of **dysentery**. Crossing the Nubian Desert was hard work. He was weak and tired, his feet bled, and his face was so swollen that he could hardly open his eyes. He finally arrived in London on June 21, 1774. It had taken him three years to get home. Once he was back in Britain, Bruce praised the city of Gondar so much that no one believed his stories. Bruce wrote his book, *Travels to Discover the Sources of the Nile*, in an attempt to convince people of his amazing journey. The book was published in 1790.

The River's Source

John Hanning Speke discovered the real source of the Nile. He was born in England in 1827, and spent some time as an officer in the British Indian army. In 1856, Speke and Richard Burton were sent to Africa by the British Royal Geographical Society. They were sent to explore eastern Africa and find out the true source of the Nile. Traveling with 132 Africans and 36 mules, the party moved inland from Zanzibar, arriving at Lake Tanganyika on February 13, 1858. Speke then traveled north on his own with about 30 men to help him. By July 30, he arrived at a stretch of water that he named after his queen—Lake Victoria. Speke thought that the lake might be the real source of the Nile and on his final expedition in 1864 he confirmed this but many people disagreed with him.

The Niger River

Five years after Bruce had finished writing *Travels to Discover the Sources of the Nile* (see previous page), another Scotsman was traveling, this time through West Africa in search of the Niger River. His name was Mungo Park and he was sent by the African Association in Britain to trace the unknown course of the Niger.

Inside West Africa

Mungo Park sailed from England on May 27, 1795, landing on the northern bank of the Gambia River 30 days later. Park made his way up the river to Pisania and stayed with a British slave trader for five months to learn the local Mandingo language. On December 2, 1795, Park set off for the Niger River with an interpreter, a servant, and a few horses. The first few days of his journey went quite well. A king gave him a guide and some provisions, and at the village of Koojar he was entertained with dances. But once the party began traveling again, their luck changed. Park was robbed twice and ended up losing most of his possessions and all of his money. In the end, he had to borrow some money from an African trader.

The Niger River

On *his first journey across West Africa, it took Park a year to reach the banks of the Niger River.*

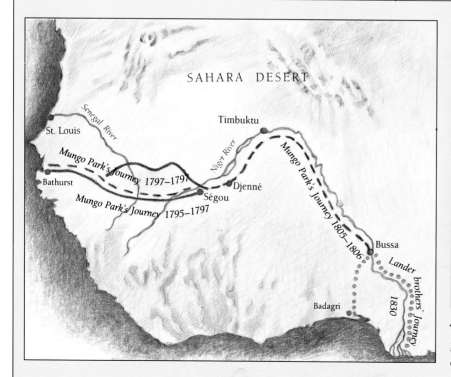

SAHARA DESERT

The *Niger is one of the world's longest rivers. It flows for 2,600 miles through several countries, including Mali.*

Into Dangerous Country

Park continued his journey eastward, and arrived in the kingdom of Ludmar on February 18, 1796. The Muslim ruler of the country, Ali, suspected that Park was a spy and imprisoned him in a hut for three months. Park was forced to travel with Ali to the towns of Bubaker and Jaraa, where he was insulted and taunted by the local people. Then, on July 1, Park escaped across the desert on an old horse. He had no money, his clothes were in rags, and he was extremely thirsty. Just as Mungo was about to give up, he arrived at a Fulani village where an old woman took pity on him and gave him some food.

An African woman gives a starving Park some broiled fish to eat.

The Glorious River

Park finally reached the northern bank of the Niger on July 7, 1796. He was refused permission to visit Ségou, a town on the southern bank, so Park decided to travel on to the city of Djenné. Sheer exhaustion prevented him from reaching the city and he decided to head back to the west coast. His return journey was just as dangerous. Suspected of being a Christian spy, he was turned away from villages. He had very little food and was forced to eat raw corn for three days. Park was attacked by robbers many times and had to swim across rivers to escape. Finally, over a year after he had reached the Niger, Park landed back on English soil.

Park's Second Journey

Park wrote a book about his travels that was published in 1799. Then, in January 1805, the British government sent him back to Africa to find out where the Niger ended. This time Park's party included 43 Europeans, but by the time he got to the Niger only 4 of them were still alive as the rest had died of fever. Park never saw the mouth of the Niger. While traveling down the river in a canoe, he was ambushed at Bussa and drowned in the river. The course of the Niger from Timbuktu to the coast was finally traced by Richard and John Lander, who sailed down the river in 1830.

Mungo Park's second journey into Africa ended in disaster. He was ambushed at Bussa and drowned.

René Caillié (right) was the first European to travel to Timbuktu and back. He made many sketches of the famous city (above), which he included in the book he wrote about his travels.

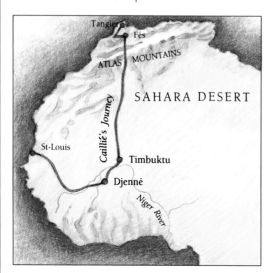

The Mystery of Timbuktu

James Bruce and Mungo Park had traveled to Africa to find the sources and **courses** of rivers. But Europeans also wanted to know about famous West African cities, particularly Timbuktu. On April 27, 1816, at the tender age of 16, René Caillié left his hometown in France to travel to the famous city.

René's First Steps

René arrived on the West African coast ten weeks later. He tried his best to join a British expedition, even walking 300 miles to meet them at Gorée. But he was so tired by the time he got there that a French soldier persuaded him to return to Guadeloupe. René worked there for a while, reading about the adventures of other explorers and longing to return to Africa. In 1818, René was back in West Africa. He joined another expedition but was unprepared for the harsh desert journey. Falling ill at Bakel, he returned to the west coast and sailed back to France.

A Third Try

René spent his time in France working for a firm of wine merchants. In 1824, just after his 24th birthday, he sailed again to West Africa. This time he decided that he would travel on his own and pretend to be an Egyptian Arab. First of all he needed to find out about the Muslim religion and so René traveled inland to live with a group of Muslims to learn as much as he could about Islam.

Timbuktu Beckons

Back in St-Louis (in Senegal), René worked as a manager of an **indigo** factory, saving all his money to buy gifts to use on his journey in exchange for food and shelter. Finally, in March 1827, René put on his Arab clothes and set off toward Timbuktu. By the time he arrived at Tiéme five months later (halfway to Timbuktu), René was suffering from **scurvy**. An old woman in the city looked after him, forcing him to drink **rice water** twice a day. René recovered slowly but it was not until January 1828 that he was ready to continue his journey. He joined a caravan on its way to the city of Djenné. From Djenné he sailed on to Timbuktu, arriving at the city on April 20, 1828.

Tuaregs are the largest group of nomads who live in the Sahara desert. They are descendants of people who originally lived in Libya over 2,000 years ago Today they number over 300,000. Tuaregs wear loose clothes to keep cool, and the men wear turbans, which they wrap around their heads and across their faces. The turban forms a veil, and only their eyes can be seen. This protects them from the desert wind and sandstorms.

René Caillié lived in a house like this when he stayed in Timbuktu.

Back to France

René was disappointed with Timbuktu. It was not as grand as he had expected but nevertheless he stayed in the city for a month before returning to France. This time he traveled with a caravan of 1,400 camels and 400 Arab merchants through the desert. Throughout the crossing René kept dreaming about water. But he made it, and by September 1828 René was in Morocco. From there he traveled on to France, arriving there in October of the same year. It had taken him almost a year to get to Timbuktu, and René had traveled over half of the 1,500-mile journey on foot. Back in Paris, René was honored by the Geographical Society of Paris and given a prize of 10,000 francs for being the first European to return from Timbuktu alive.

Earlier Visitors

Leo Africanus (1492–1552) was born in Granada. He was a Muslim who spent time traveling around Africa and the Middle East. In 1518, he was captured by pirates and taken to Rome (Italy). Pope Leo X was so impressed with the traveler's knowledge that he set him free, converted him to Christianity, and baptized him "Leo." Leo Africanus decided to travel to West Africa. He wanted to see Timbuktu because he had heard that all the roofs there were made out of gold. After visiting the city, Leo returned to Italy, where he wrote a book about his travels.

Barth made sketches of all the cities he visited. This one was drawn by him in the mid-1800s and shows the city of Kano.

The Traveling Scholar

Twenty-five years after René Caillié's journey, another European explorer visited the city of Timbuktu. He was a German scholar named Heinrich Barth. Born in Hamburg in 1821, Barth had traveled widely around the Mediterranean before the British government asked him to join an expedition in central Africa to encourage trade and to suppress the slave trade in the interior.

The Journey Begins

The expedition left Tripoli on March 24, 1850, and made slow progress across the desert. In August, the party escaped a band of robbers, who managed to steal a few of their camels. By the time the expedition arrived at Tintellust in September, everyone was in need of a rest. Barth spent a month there before setting out on his own for Agades. Agades was an important starting point on one of the trade routes in the desert. No European had ever been there. Barth spent three weeks in the city, walking around with his pencil and sketchbook and visiting the mosques. Next Barth visited Gobir, Kano, and Kukawa, and by mid-June he had reached the Benue River. Barth managed to cross the river with his horses, camels, and luggage and continued until he got to the town of Yola. But the king there refused to let him stay in the city, so Barth returned to Kukawa.

Tunis

Tripoli

Murzuk

Barth's Journey

SAHARA DESERT

Agadès

Timbuktu

Kano

Niger River

Benue River

Yola

Traveling with Bandits

Barth spent several months traveling to places near Kukawa. Then, on September 11, he left for Kanem. He met a group of Arab robbers along the way and traveled with them for three weeks. In that time, the robbers stole 300 cows, 1,500 sheep and goats, and 15 camels. Barth returned to Kukawa in February 1852 and left a month later for Massénya.

On to Timbuktu

Barth spent three months in Kukawa before leaving for Timbuktu on November 25, 1853. He stopped at Sebba for two days to allow his camels to rest. Afterward, Barth hired 11 donkeys to carry his luggage to Timbuktu. Because the area was very dangerous for Christians, Barth pretended to be an important Muslim visitor to escape attack.

Home to Germany

Barth stayed in Timbuktu for about seven months. On his return journey, he followed the Niger River up to Gogo, then continued through the desert, arriving at Fezzan on July 6, 1854. The people of the town welcomed him and congratulated him on his successful trip. He finally sailed to Malta and then to London, arriving on September 6, 1855. Barth wrote about his travels and died in Berlin in 1865.

Barth visited Agades, a city in the middle of the Sahara Desert. The mosque in the picture is over 700 years old.

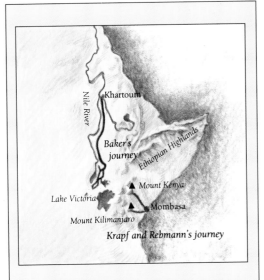

Early Missionaries and Explorers

Ludwig Krapf and Johannes Rebmann were German missionaries who explored southeastern Africa. Rebmann saw the snowcapped mountain of Kilimanjaro in 1849 and Krapf was the first European to see Mount Kenya (1848). The journeys of Krapf and Rebmann inspired and excited other explorers with their sightings of these mountains. The British Royal Geographical Society sent Richard Burton and John Hanning Speke (see page 29) on an expedition to find the source of the Nile (1856–1858). Later, from 1860–1863, Speke and James Grant were the first Europeans to go to the African kingdoms of Buganda and Bunyoro (see pages 20–21).

Samuel and Florence Baker were a husband and wife team who led antislavery expeditions into Africa during the late 1800s.

Routes to the Coast

Perhaps the greatest explorer of them all was Dr. David Livingstone, a Scottish doctor and missionary, who spent 28 years traveling around Africa. He arrived at Cape Town in southern Africa in March 1841, on his way to the Christian Mission at Kuruman founded by Robert Moffat, whose daughter Mary he married. The young couple spent the years that followed building three more mission stations, each one farther north. The Livingstones were discouraged by their failure to convert the local people to Christianity and the hostility of the local **Boer** farmers. They decided to explore farther afield.

First Expeditions

On June 1, 1849, Livingstone and some of his friends set out across the Kalahari Desert to find Lake Ngami on the northern edge of the desert. They took an African guide with them and it was so hot that the party could only travel at night. It took them two whole months to get to the lake. The next expedition Livingstone made was to meet the king of the Makololo people, who was called Sebetwane. This time Livingstone decided to take his family with him and they almost perished during the hazardous journey. His sufferings were rewarded though, for Sebetwane welcomed them and was very friendly.

The next time Livingstone set out, he traveled without his family, whom he sent back to England. He wanted to establish a mission station farther inland and arrived at Linyanti, the capital of the Makololo people, on May 23, 1853. Sebetwane had already died but his son, Sekelutu, was just as friendly toward him. A month later, accompanied by Sekelutu and many Makololo people, Livingstone began his search for a suitable site. The party sailed down the Zambezi River in canoes, passing herds of buffalo and listening to lions roaring in the distance. But Livingstone failed to find a site and his party returned to Linyanti.

This *scene of central Africa's Victoria Falls was drawn by Thomas Baines.*

On to the Coast

Livingstone then decided to try and find a route from Linyanti to the west coast. Sekelutu gave him 27 men to accompany him to Luanda on the coast. The expedition left on November 11, 1853, traveling up the Zambezi River in a northwesterly direction. Livingstone was attacked constantly by fever, but refused to stop the journey. The men carried him, cutting grass for him to sleep on at night and cooking all his food. When they arrived at the Portuguese trading station of Cassange, Livingstone was given some new clothes and a guide to take him on to the coast. Three weeks later, on May 31, 1854, a tired and disheveled Livingstone arrived at the coastal town of Luanda, the present-day capital of Angola. A ship's doctor treated his fever and dysentery, and Livingstone remained in the town for four months until he recovered his strength. On September 20, 1854, he began his return journey to Linyanti, arriving there a year later.

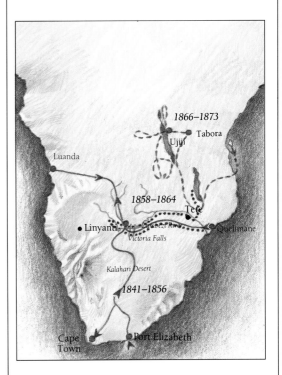

The journeys of David Livingstone

British society was impressed by David Livingstone's expeditions into Africa. This popular photograph was sold to an adoring general public. Livingstone stands by a globe to signify his travels. On the chair rests the famous hat that he wore on his journeys.

Livingstone almost lost his life when he was attacked by a lion.

East and England

Livingstone spent two months writing letters and recording his geographical discoveries. He was unhappy with the route he had found to the west coast because it was already being used by Arab slave traders. Livingstone decided to try and find an alternative link to the east. On November 3, 1855, he set off with 114 Makololo people. The expedition sailed down the Zambezi River, visiting the magnificent Victoria Falls on the way. Livingstone arrived at the East African port of Quelimane on May 20, 1856, after traveling partly by river and partly by land. He was the first European to cross Africa from coast to coast.

Finding Trading Routes

When Livingstone arrived back in England in 1856, he was greeted as a hero. The Royal Geographical Society gave him one of its two gold medals and he was received by Queen Victoria. He traveled the country lecturing on his experiences and against the slave trade.

Livingstone sailed along the rivers of Africa in this steamboat called the Ma Robert.

The British government decided to send him back to Africa in 1858, to find out more about the rivers of the continent so that they could be used as routes for taking trading goods into the heart of Africa. This time he explored some of the Zambezi area and villages around Lake Malawi. He returned to England in 1864.

Livingstone's last journey was sponsored by the Royal Geographical Society in London. His aim was to find the source of the Nile, which had been argued about for many years. Livingstone arrived at Zanzibar in January 1866, and traveled inland to Lake Malawi with about 60 people. The 54-year-old Livingstone was not as strong as he had once been. He suffered from bouts of fever throughout the expedition and by the middle of February was suffering from **rheumatic fever**. Livingstone sent letters to Zanzibar asking for supplies to be sent to Ujiji on Lake Tanganyika. He planned to travel there to collect them. By the time he arrived there on October 23, 1871, all the supplies had been stolen. Livingstone was devastated, and as his health deteriorated, he prayed for a miracle. That miracle came in the form of Henry Morton Stanley.

Stanley Arrives

No one in Europe had heard from Livingstone for over four years, and everyone thought he was dead. The American newspaper the *New York Herald* decided to send one of its journalists, Henry Stanley, to Africa to find Livingstone. Stanley got to Zanzibar early in 1871 and organized the biggest expedition yet—two boats, a caravan of camels and donkeys, and 200 porters. Stanley set off across the humid **savanna** of East Africa and quickly covered 210 miles. Arriving at Ujiji late in the year, Stanley greeted Livingstone with the famous words, "Dr. Livingstone, I presume?" Stanley spent four months with Livingstone, and they explored Lake Tanganyika together. But Livingstone refused to return with Stanley to England.

Livingstone fell very ill on his last expedition, and the Africans in his party had to carry him on a stretcher.

Livingstone's Last Journey

Stanley escorted Livingstone as far as Tabora. After resting there for three months, Livingstone set out again on his last journey. He soon started suffering from dysentery, yet he continued his travels, marching toward Lake Tanganyika. By April, Livingstone could hardly walk and had to be carried by his companions. In May 1873, the great explorer died. His embalmed body was carried back to the coast by his African friends and given to the British. Their journey of 1,600 miles was a remarkable feat. It took them nine months to complete the journey.

Stanley finally found Livingstone at Ujiji, on the shores of Lake Tanganyika.

Stanley's Journeys

Henry Morton Stanley made three important expeditions across Africa. The first was to find Livingstone in 1871, the second was to finish Livingstone's explorations in central Africa (1874–1877) and the third was to rescue **Emin Pasha**, who was under siege from a hostile army.

On his second journey, Stanley crossed Africa from east to west, proving Speke to be right in his discovery of the source of the Nile River at Lake Victoria (see page 29). Then Stanley crossed Lake Tanganyika and traced the route of the Zaire River to its mouth. Stanley's story of a great inland waterway leading into the heart of Africa aroused European interest as people saw a way they could transport goods for trading into the country.

On his third trip, Stanley crossed Africa from west to east. He saw the Ruwenzori Mountains and recorded what he saw of the geography of the continent.

After Livingstone's death, Stanley continued his exploration of central Africa.

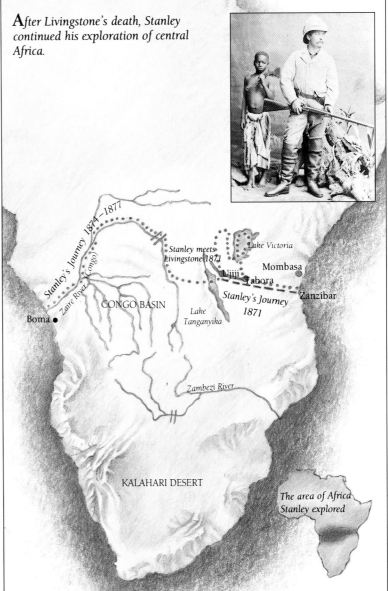

Stanley's Journey 1874–1877

Zaire River (Congo)

Stanley meets Livingstone 1871

Lake Victoria

Mombasa

Ujiji · Tabora

Zanzibar

Stanley's Journey 1871

CONGO BASIN

Lake Tanganyika

Boma

Zambezi River

KALAHARI DESERT

The area of Africa Stanley explored

7 Modern Times

Africa Is Colonized

Many missionaries traveled to Africa to convert people to Christianity. This is a mission school in the Congo c. 1900.

Once Europeans knew about the rivers of Africa, they used boats such as these to transport goods around the continent. Traveling by water was much faster than traveling by land.

By the late 1800s, European explorers had traveled around almost all of the African continent. They had laid down a map of rivers, lakes, and mountains and met many African people. Explorers published books in their own countries about their journeys, the wealth of raw materials in Africa, and the benefits of trade with the continent.

As the 19th century progressed, the attitude of the Europeans changed. They were not content to just explore and trade. They wanted to control the new, lucrative African markets.

The Scramble for Africa

In 1884, the European powers held an international conference in Berlin. It was called the West African Conference. During the meeting, the European powers decided who would control which parts of the continent. Thirty years later, nearly all of Africa had been colonized. The "scramble" for Africa was over.

The Missionaries

Along with trade and politics, religion also played a major role in shaping the development of Africa. Using the newly developed steamships to travel up the rivers of Africa into the interior, Christian missionaries penetrated farther than ever before. They also used a new drug, quinine, to help fight malaria, a **fatal** disease.

Gold mining in South Africa in 1888

Resistance in Africa

Resistance to colonization was widespread throughout Africa. The European powers had to fight many bloody battles with the armies of existing African nations to take over the continent. It was generally one-sided. The Europeans had machine guns, which were much better weapons than the outdated guns of the Africans.

However, there were notable successes for some African kingdoms. The Zulus wiped out an entire British regiment in 1879 in South Africa. They had old-fashioned weapons but used the element of surprise and weight of numbers to defeat the British.

The Partition of Africa

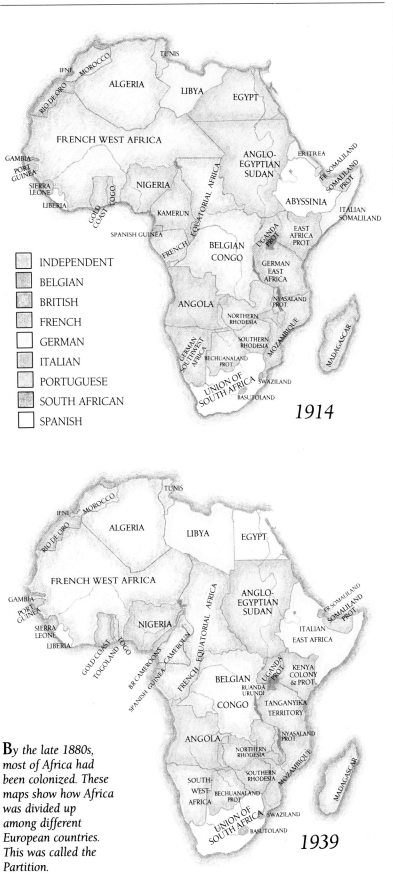

INDEPENDENT
BELGIAN
BRITISH
FRENCH
GERMAN
ITALIAN
PORTUGUESE
SOUTH AFRICAN
SPANISH

1914

By the late 1880s, most of Africa had been colonized. These maps show how Africa was divided up among different European countries. This was called the Partition.

1939

41

Africa Today

Africa was controlled by European countries for many years. They imposed their own forms of government and even imposed their own national boundaries, which cut across traditional and natural divides. After World War II ended in 1945, Africans once again began to fight for their independence.

Inherited Problems

Some of Africa's current problems were inherited from her colonial years. For example, before Africa was taken over, there were many different groups living within it. European colonial powers divided Africa up. They did so for their own reasons, ignoring the different cultures and languages within the continent. After independence, some of the different groups that found themselves living in the newly formed countries quarreled with each other for many different reasons and this sometimes led to **civil war**.

One of the reasons why some African states have suffered from wars since independence is because of the artificial boundaries placed upon countries by the colonialists. This picture of destruction in Eritrea shows the damage caused by such a war.

The first prime minister of Kenya, Jomo Kenyatta

Africa for Africans

A group of important African leaders from around the world held a conference in Manchester, England, in 1945. Among those who attended were Jomo Kenyatta from Kenya, George Padmore from the West Indies, Dr. W. E. B. Du Bois from the United States, and Kwame Nkrumah from the Gold Coast. At the meeting, they all decided that Africans should be allowed to elect their own governments. Twelve years later, Kwame Nkrumah led his country to independence and the country became known as Ghana. In 1963, after years of fierce guerrilla fighting, Kenya became an independent country under Jomo Kenyatta.

By the 1960s, almost all of Africa was free. However, the legacies of European rule caused many problems for the new African countries.

W. E. B. Du Bois was an American historian and sociologist (1868–1963). He devoted much of his life to the struggle against racial prejudice in America and Africa.

Modern-Day Africa

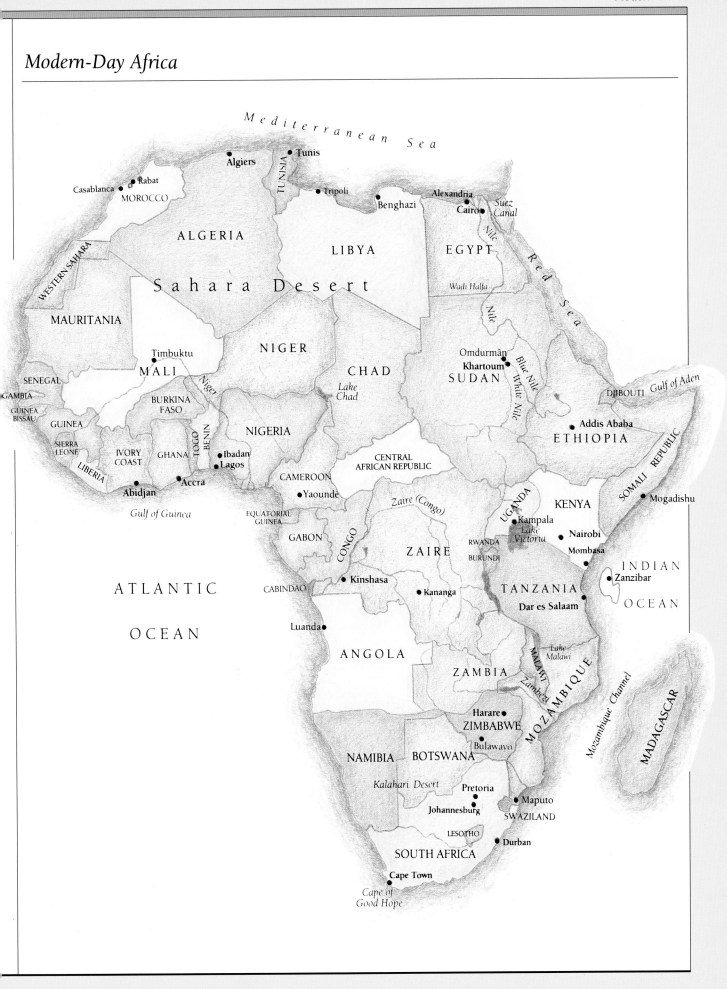

Africa has suffered from bad periods of drought in recent years.

Food Shortages

One of the major obstacles for some African countries is drought. This severe lack of water leads to food shortages in some instances. Chad, Ethiopia, Sudan, and Somalia have all suffered terrible droughts recently, which, if combined with civil war, devastate the economy. The causes of drought are complicated. Some parts of the continent are prone to water shortages. Traditional farming could cope with the problem: If one area of land was barren, people moved their cattle on. Putting up national boundaries has made this more difficult.

Many scientists now believe that recent changes in the climate in Africa (which have led to less rainfall) are due to pollution in the world's atmosphere—most of which comes from Europe and North America.

Economic Problems

During the colonial period, crops such as cotton and peanuts were grown to supply European markets. The terms of trade were never in the African farmer's interest. European merchants along the coast bought the crops at low prices and sold goods from Europe for high prices. The Africans were paid less for what they sold and had to pay a lot for the goods they bought. When European rule ended, many African nations were experiencing an economic crisis and had to get loans from banks throughout the world. These loans are still being paid off today. This often means that African countries have to grow and sell crops to earn money to pay off the debts rather than keep the crops for food.

Modern Visitors and New Explorers

In spite of these problems, Africa remains a vast, complex, and beautiful continent. It attracts millions of visitors every year, many of whom join wildlife safaris or expeditions that trek across the harsh Sahara Desert. Others visit the continent's numerous beaches, soaking up the sun or exploring the famous relics of ancient kingdoms.

Apart from tourists, Africa also attracts the new explorers: archaeologists and anthropologists. Anthropologists study the way people live and how they have adapted to new circumstances and conditions. Archaeologists study the objects and remains of ancient peoples to find out how they lived thousands of years ago.

Human Bones

One modern explorer who did a great deal of work in eastern Africa was Louis Leakey. Born in Kenya in 1903, Leakey started hunting for the bones of ancient humans in the 1920s. This search was taken up by many archaeologists eager to discover information about the roots of mankind. Mary Leakey also worked in Kenya and Tanzania as an archaeologist. She had married Leakey in 1936 and accompanied him on many of his trips. In 1959, she found the skull of a humanlike creature at Olduvai Gorge (see box). It is called *Zinjanthropus* and lived about one and a half million years ago. In 1962, around Tanzania, Leakey found the remains of species that had an apelike jaw. He thought the species must have lived there over 14 million years ago. Later on, he found the bones of one of the first human beings at Olduvai Gorge. The Leakeys' son, Richard, is also interested in human remains. He found the skull of an advanced type of **prehistoric** man called *Homo erectus* in 1975. It was found at Lake Turkana and is about one and a half million years old. Because of the Leakey family's work, people now believe that the first human beings **evolved** in Africa.

A Fertile Desert

Other archaeologists have spent time hunting in the western part of Africa. Henry Lhote discovered rock paintings around the Niger River. Some archaeologists concern themselves with ancient sculptures and paintings in order to discover more about Africa's rich ancient cultures. Dr. Ekpo Eyo has found many sculptures and paintings in Nigeria. Working with British, German, and American archaeologists, he has shown these beautiful ancient works in museums all over the world.

Raymond Mauny worked in the Sahara Desert. He found ancient rock pictures drawn by the people who lived there over 4,000 years ago. These paintings depict rivers and animal life running across the now barren desert.

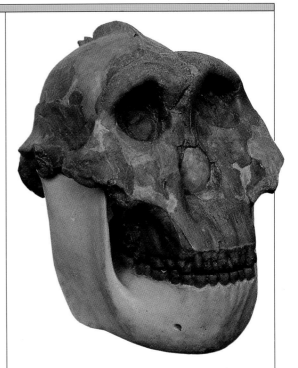

The prehistoric skull found by Mary Leakey at Olduvai Gorge

Olduvai Gorge

Olduvai Gorge (in modern-day Tanzania) has been one of the most important archaeological sites in the world since the late 19th century. The gorge is 300 feet deep and several miles long. The walls of the gorge have been investigated by geologists hunting fossils and studying the structure and history of the earth itself.

During their excavations in the 1930s, the Leakeys found pebble tools used by the first human beings. In 1958–1959, the Leakeys found the remains of prehistoric animals from the same early human culture—including sheep that were the size of cart horses and pigs as large as rhinoceroses.

Africa	Europe	Other
8000 B.C. Farming begins along the upper Nile.	c.6500 B.C. Farming begins in Greece and spreads to other areas of Europe.	9000 B.C. Hunters spread throughout North and South America.
c.6000 Use of iron begins in Egypt. c.3000 Ancient Egypt founded.	c.3000 Use of copper spreads throughout Europe.	c.2500 The horse is domesticated in central Asia.
c.2000 The Saharan climate begins to get drier.	c.1600 Mycenaean civilization begins in Greece.	c.1500 The use of iron begins in Turkey. c.1200 The Jewish religion emerges.
c.500 The Nok culture is founded in West Africa.	510 The Roman Republic is founded.	c.650 Iron is being used in China. c.230 The Great Wall of China is built.
A.D. 1 The camel is introduced into North Africa at about this time.	A.D. 43 The Roman Empire invades Britain.	A.D. 30 Death of Jesus Christ. Spread of Christianity begins.
300s The Ghanaian Empire is founded in West Africa.	117 The Roman Empire is at its greatest extent.	c.320–480 Golden age of Hinduism in India.
400 Bantu-speaking peoples reach the east coast.	c.542 Bubonic plague spreads through Europe.	622 Mohammad founds the religion of Islam in Arabia.
900s Arabs begin to settle along the east coast.	959 The Unification of England.	935 The text of the Quran finished. 960 Sung dynasty in China.
c1200s The rise of the Mali Empire. c1200s Great Zimbabwe is founded.	1066 The Normans conquer England.	c.1000 The Vikings colonize Greenland and travel to America.
1352–54 Ibn Battuta travels to the Mali Empire.	1340s The bubonic plague continues to spread throughout Europe.	1368 Ming dynasty in China.
1482 The Portuguese build Elmina Castle along the Gold Coast (Ghana).	1492 The first globe is made in Germany by Martin Behaim.	1492 Christopher Columbus reaches the Americas.
1530s The European slave trade begins across the Atlantic Ocean.	1532 John Calvin starts the Protestant movement in France.	1526 The founding of the Mogul Empire in India.
1652 The Dutch found Cape Colony in South Africa.	1618 The Thirty Years War of religion starts.	1607 The first English settlement is founded in America (Virginia).
1680 Founding of the Rozvi Empire in Zimbabwe.	1667 The French begin to expand under Louis XIV.	1644 Manchu dynasty in China.
c.1700s The rise of Asante power.	1707 England and Scotland unite.	1699 The French establish the colony of Louisiana in America.
c.1700s The rise of Buganda.	1756 The Seven Years War begins. c.1760 The Age of Enlightenment.	1775 The American Revolution begins.
c.1700s The Masai spread throughout East Africa.	1789 The French Revolution begins.	1789 George Washington becomes the first president of the United States.
c.1700s The European exploration of Africa begins.	1807 The slave trade is abolished in Britain.	1857 The Indian Mutiny.
1835–37 The Great Trek of the Boers in South Africa inland from the Cape.	1884–85 The West African Conference is held in Berlin (Germany).	1861 The American Civil War begins.
c.1915 Africa continues to be divided up among the European powers.	1914–18 World War I.	1917 The U.S. enters World War I.
1935–41 Italian occupation of Ethiopia.	1939–45 World War II.	1941 The U.S. enters World War II.
1960s Thirty-six African colonies become independent.	1961 The Berlin Wall is built in Germany.	1961 John F. Kennedy becomes president of the U.S. 1963 John F. Kennedy is assassinated.
1975 Break up of Portuguese African Empire. 1976 The Soweto uprising in South Africa.	1972 The European Community gains more members.	1965–73 The U.S. is involved in the Vietnam War.
1980 Zimbabwe becomes independent.	1985 Mikhail Gorbachev becomes the leader of the Soviet Union.	1981 Ronald Reagan becomes the U.S. president.
1990 Nelson Mandela is released. 1991 Apartheid begins to break apart in South Africa.	1989 The Berlin Wall is destroyed. 1990 East and West Germany are united. 1991 Boris Yeltsin becomes leader of Russia.	1989 Tiananmen Square massacre in China. 1993 Bill Clinton becomes the U.S. president.

Glossary

A

acacia tree: a beautiful, thorny gum tree found all over Africa.

B

barter: when goods are bartered it means that they are exchanged for other goods of the same value.

bearers: Africans who traveled with European explorers and helped transport supplies.

Berbers: a large group of Africans who live in North Africa.

Boer: a descendant of the Dutch people who came to South Africa in the 17th century.

C

caravan: a group of merchants, camels, and goods traveling across a desert.

civil war: a war in which people from within the same country fight each other.

colony: land that is taken over by settlers from another part of the world and ruled by them is called a colony.

consul: a British official responsible for protecting British interests in a foreign country.

coral: is found on the bottom of the sea. It is a hard substance rather like bone and is made over many years from things like bone, shells, and skeletons left in the sea by various animals. Coral can be found in many beautiful colors.

course: the exact route of a river.

D

dhow: a type of ship originally built by the Arabs, most often used for carrying trading goods.

dysentery: an infection caused by bacteria or similar germs, involving extreme diarrhea, digestive upsets, and pains in various parts of the body.

E

Emin Pasha: (1849–1892) a German explorer and doctor appointed by the British general Gordon to be medical officer and then governor of a British province in Africa. Emin Pasha became isolated by hostile Arab forces and was rescued by Stanley in 1889.

ethnic: a particular group of people who can be identified by their culture, language, dress, and customs.

evolution: the slow development that changed apes into human beings.

F

fast: a period of time when someone does not eat any food.

fatal: something that results in death, such as an accident or a disease.

Fulani: a group of Africans who live south of the Sahara Desert in West Africa. They originated around present-day Senegal, and now number about five million.

H

headwaters: the highest part of a stream or river. The water closest to the source of the river.

hectare: an area of land the size of 2.47 acres.

humanitarians: people who work to help mankind.

I

illegitimate: someone whose parents are not married when they are born is illegitimate.

indigo: a violet blue dye that is taken from the leaves of the indigo plant.

Industrial Revolution: a period of social and economic change beginning in Britain in the 1760s. It involved the change from working mainly in homes and on farms to working in factories and using large machines.

industrialists: people who own factories that manufacture goods.

interior: the name that was given by Europeans to the unknown middle of Africa.

K

kola nuts: a seed of the kola tree which contains caffeine. Caffeine is an important ingredient of coffee.

M

migration: the movement of a community of people or animals from one place to another either to settle permanently or to visit for a certain period of time.

millet: a type of grass that is grown for food.

missionary: someone who tries to convert people from one religion to another.

monsoon: a strong wind that occurs in Asia. The monsoon blows southwest during summer and northeast the rest of the year.

Muslim: follower of a religion called Islam, which was founded in Arabia in 622 (see page 9).

P

pagan: someone who is not a Jew, a Christian, or a Muslim.

palm oil: oil that is extracted from oil palm trees. The oil was used in factory machines.

plantation: a large area of land where crops such as rubber and sugar are grown for sale.

prehistoric: something that dates from a time before history as we know it began. The dinosaurs are prehistoric animals.

provincial ruler: someone who rules over an area outside a city or empire.

R

Ramadan: a month of the year when Muslims do not eat until after sunset.

raw materials: the basic, untreated materials (e.g., rubber or sugar) that are used to manufacture other products.

rheumatic fever: a disease that makes people suffer from fever and painful joints.

rice water: water that has had rice boiled in it. Once the rice has been boiled, it is removed and the water is drunk as an aid to recovery from illness.

S

savanna: the name given to a region of grassland with a few scattered trees. The savanna is very hot.

scholar: a student of a particular area, subject, or discipline.

scurvy: a disease caused by the body not having enough vitamin C. Sufferers have dry skin and swollen gums.

source: the origin of a river or stream; the place where it starts.

T

tropical diseases: diseases that are found in the tropical regions of the world, such as malaria.

Z

Zimbabwean Plateau: the name given to the geographical feature that Great Zimbabwe was built upon. A plateau is a flat area of land that is raised above the rest of the land in the area.

Index

Numbers in **bold** indicate an illustration. Words in **bold** are in the glossary on page 47.